THE UNOFFICIAL GREATEST MOMENTS IN WORLD CUP HISTORY | COLOURING THE BEAUTIFUL GAME

SAN RAFAEL • LOS ANGELES • LONDON

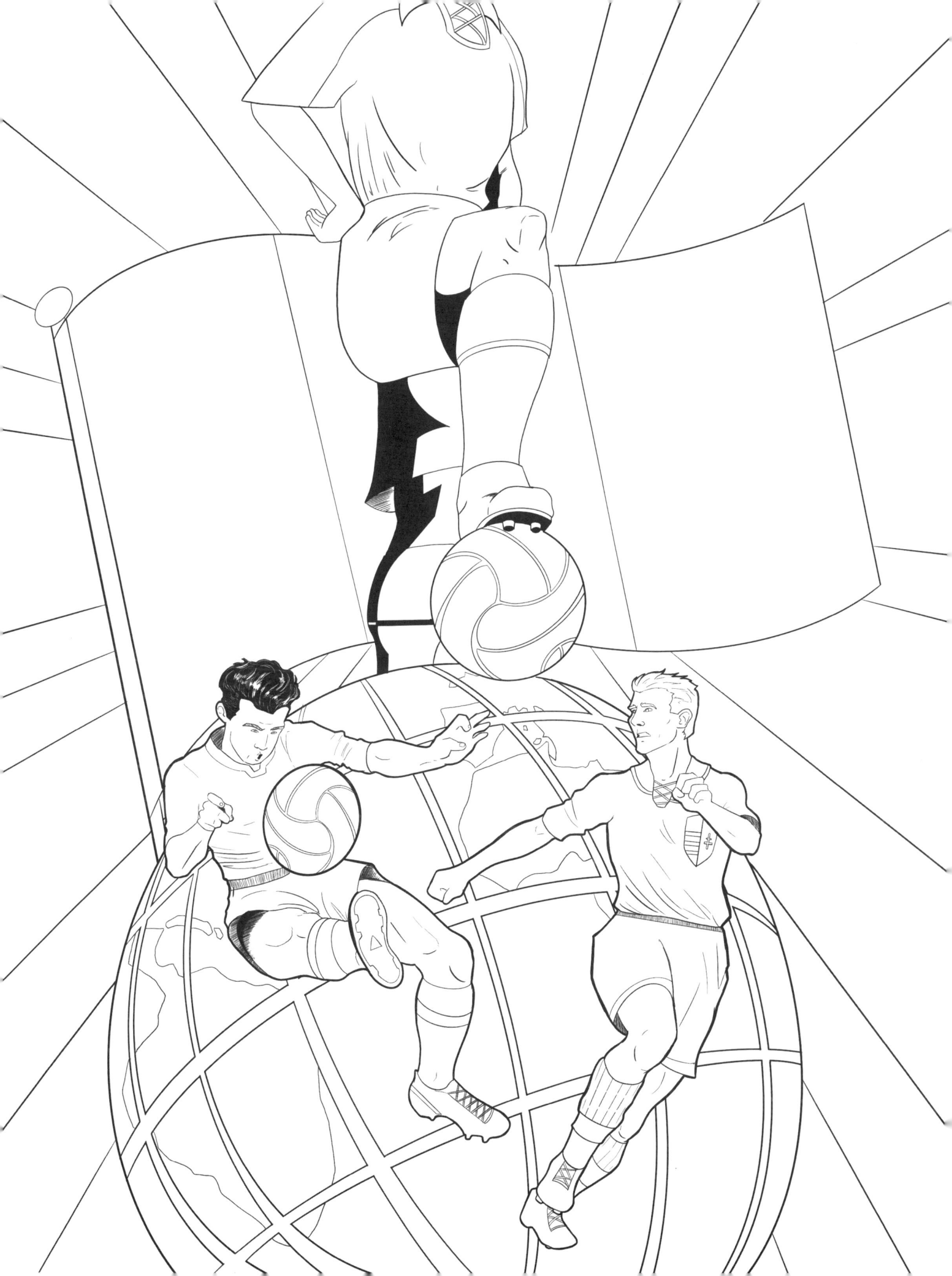

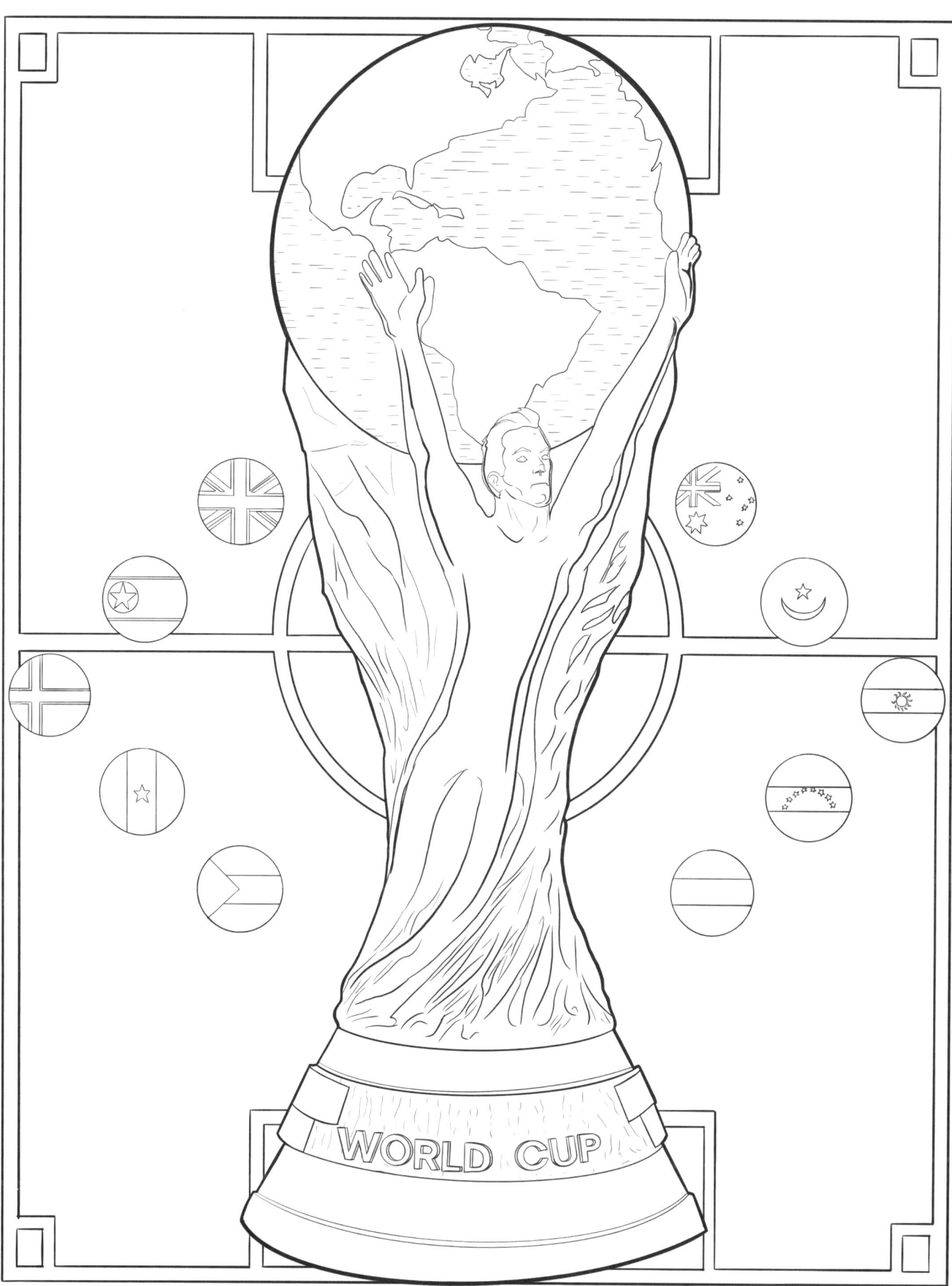

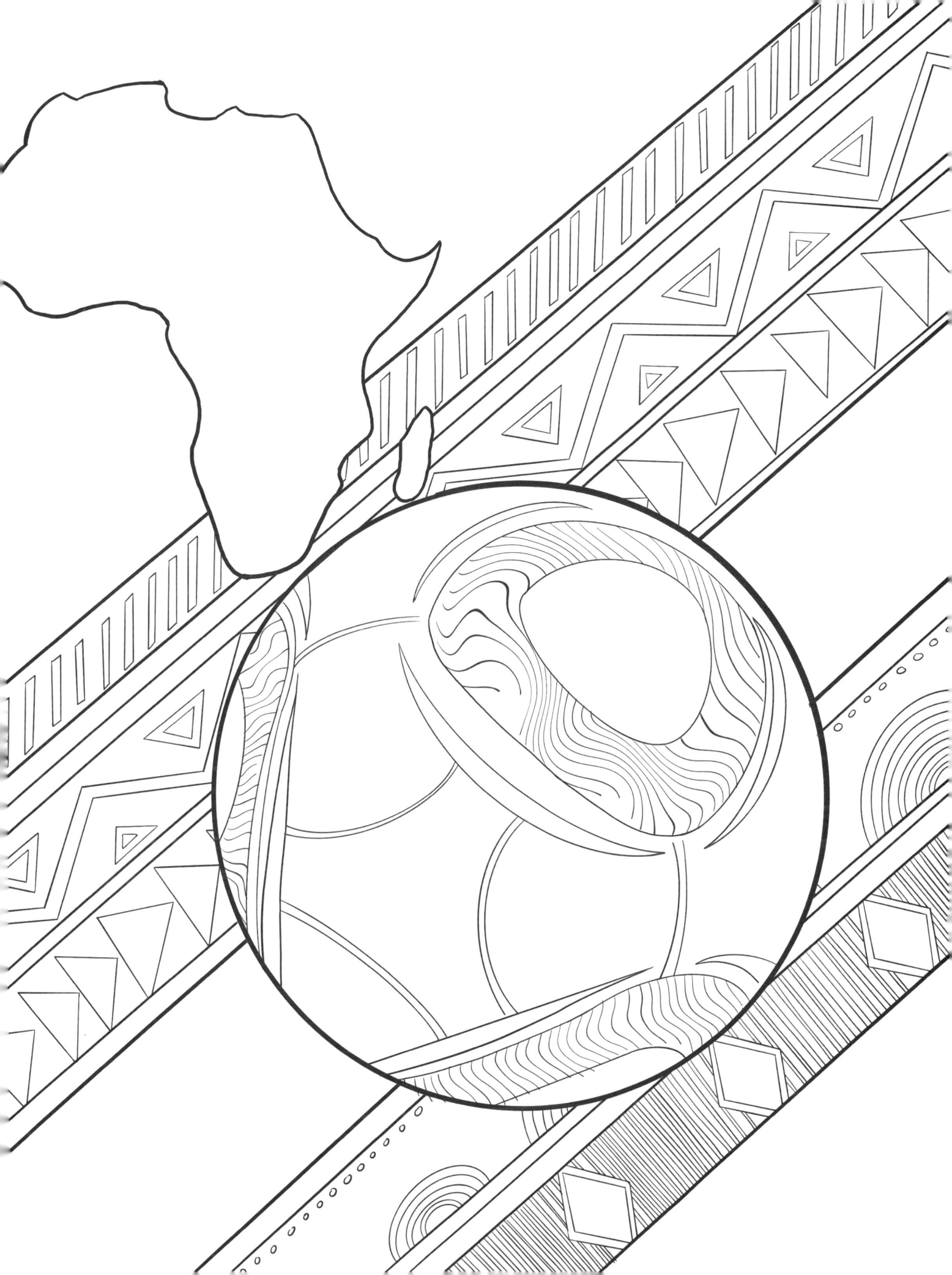

PO Box 3088
San Rafael, CA 94912
www.insighteditions.com
Find us on Facebook: www.facebook.com/InsightEditions
Follow us on Instagram: @insighteditions

All rights reserved. Published by Insight Editions, San Rafael, California, in 2026.

No part of this book may be reproduced in any form without written permission from the publisher.

ISBN: 979-8-3374-0385-4

Publisher: Raoul Goff
SVP, Group Publisher: Vanessa Lopez
VP, Manufacturing: Alix Nicholaeff
Publishing Director: Mike Degler
Editorial Director: Jennifer Sims
Creative Director: Josh Baker
Art Director: Catherine San Juan
Junior Designer: Samuel Louie
Editor: Alecsander Zapata
Managing Editor: Nora Milman
Production Manager: Tiffani Patterson
Strategic Production Planner: Lina s Palma-Temena

Illustrations by Sam Camejo

Insight Editions, in association with Roots of Peace, will plant two trees for each tree used in the manufacturing of this book. Roots of Peace is an internationally renowned humanitarian organization dedicated to eradicating land mines worldwide and converting war-torn lands into productive farms and wildlife habitats. Roots of Peace will plant two million fruit and nut trees in Afghanistan and provide farmers there with the skills and support necessary for sustainable land use.

Manufactured in China by Insight Editions

10 9 8 7 6 5 4 3 2 1